8
2x 2/11 ✓ 5/11
✓ 10/09

PO ✓

D0772724

WITHDRAWN

Going to Work ANIMAL EDITION · Going to Work ANIMAL EDITION · Going to Work ANIMAL EDITION · Going to Work AL EDITI
ANIMAL EDITION · Going to Work ANIMAL EDITION · Going to Work ANIMAL EDITION · to Work
Going to Work ANIMAL EDITION · Going to Work ANIMAL EDITION · Going to Work
ANIMAL EDITION · Going to Work ANIMAL EDITION · Going to Work

Going To Work
ANIMAL EDITION

Service Animals

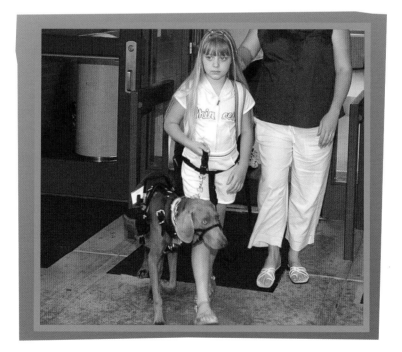

ABDO
Publishing Company

Buddy **Book by**
Julie Murray

VISIT US AT
www.abdopublishing.com

Published by ABDO Publishing Company, 8000 West 78th Street, Edina, Minnesota 55439.

Printed in the United States.

Coordinating Series Editor: Rochelle Baltzer
Editor: Sarah Tieck
Contributing Editor: Marcia Zappa
Graphic Design: Maria Hosley
Cover Photograph: *AP Photo:* Frank Anderson/Lexington Herald-Leader
Interior Photographs/Illustrations: *AP Photo:* AP Photo (p. 9), David Dick/Daily Record (p. 27), Gavin Fogg/PA Wire URN:6384678/Press Association via AP Images (p. 5), Marc F. Henning/The Daily Times (p. 23), Bob Jordan (p. 5, 26), Steven King/Casa Grande Dispatch (p. 11), Steve Kohls/The Brainerd Dispatch (p. 18), Charles Krupa (p. 13), Mike Lawrence/The Gleaner (p. 29), Jacquelyn Martin (p. 7), Eric Risberg (p. 23), Steven Senne (p. 25), Tim Shafter (p. 17), Richard Vogel (pp. 21, 22); *Getty Images:* Melanie Stetson Freeman/The Christian Science Monitor via Getty Images (p. 5); *iStockPhoto:* andres balcazar (p. 15), Doctor_bass (p. 15); *Library of Congress* (p. 9); *Photos.com:* Jupiter Images (p. 19); *Wikipedia.com* (p. 10, 14).

Library of Congress Cataloging-in-Publication Data

Murray, Julie, 1969-
  Service animals / Julie Murray.
    p. cm. -- (Going to work. Animal edition)
  ISBN 978-1-60453-564-8
  1. Working animals--Juvenile literature. I. Title.

SF172.M87 2009
636.088'6--dc22

2008040975

Contents

Animals At Work

Going to work is an important part of life. At work, people use their skills to accomplish tasks and earn money.

Animals can have jobs, too. Many times, they complete tasks that human workers can't. They can change people's lives.

Some work as service animals. They act as helpers for people with disabilities. This is worthwhile work.

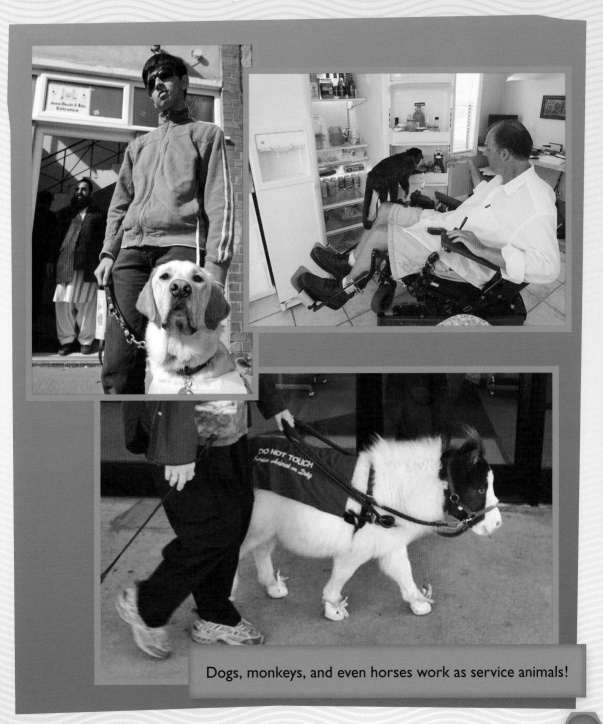

Dogs, monkeys, and even horses work as service animals!

Helping Out

Service animals are specially trained workers. They help people with everyday activities.

Service animals do certain tasks for their **partners**. For example, capuchin monkeys can get their partners a drink. And, hearing dogs can warn their partners of a smoke alarm.

Service animals can go places animals aren't normally allowed.

HISTORY LESSON

The first record of service animals was in Germany. Dogs helped **veterans** who had lost their eyesight in **World War I**.

In 1927, an article by Dorothy Harrison Eustis appeared in *The Saturday Evening Post*. In it, Eustis described how the Germans trained dogs for the blind. This got the attention of Americans.

In 1929, Eustis started The Seeing Eye. This group provides German shepherds, Labrador retrievers, golden retrievers, and boxers to blind people.

Frank's dog, Buddy, was the first known U.S. guide dog for the blind.

Morris Frank, a blind man from Tennessee, read Eustis's article. He contacted her. Together, Eustis and Frank trained a German shepherd in Switzerland. In 1928, Frank returned to the United States with his guide dog, Buddy.

Today, most guide dog trainers receive about three years of training. They help dogs and their partners learn to move through common settings, such as busy streets or stores.

Working Together

Service animals are not pets. They aid people who have **physical** and **mental** disabilities.

Each animal receives special training. Trainers teach animals to follow commands and complete simple tasks. This can take years!

Trainers teach monkeys to be useful, helpful companions.

In The World

Many service animals wear special **harnesses** or vests to help people recognize them. Their work is protected by laws. So, they can go where their **partners** go.

Service animals must pay attention to their work. People should not bother them when they are working in public places.

DO NOT PET ME I AM WORKING

Touching, feeding, or making noises at service animals interrupts important work.

Service animals go into stores, restaurants, or offices with their partners.

15

Eyes And Ears

Dogs are the most common service animal. Guide dogs aid blind people. They are their **partner**'s eyes in the world! A guide dog may help its partner safely cross a busy street.

Some service dogs help people with other **physical** problems. **Seizure** dogs **alert** their partners or get help when it's needed. One dog even telephoned for help!

Guide dogs help their partners know when to stop walking. Sometimes, they disobey a command to keep their partners safe.

Service dogs wear different harnesses for work and play. This helps them know how to behave.

Some dogs work with people who are **deaf** or have trouble hearing. Many kinds of dogs work as hearing guides.

Most hearing dogs train for four to eight months. Then, they are placed with people. Trainers teach the new **partners** how to work with their service dogs.

Hearing dogs recognize sounds such as doorbells, telephones, and alarms. Then, they notify their partners.

Helping Hands

Capuchin monkeys are another type of service animal. These smart, curious animals have thumbs. So, they can easily pick up objects. Capuchin monkeys often help people who are disabled by an **injury** to the **spine**.

Most monkey helpers attend a special school. There, they learn to help people with everyday activities. These include turning off lights, flipping pages of a book, and opening and closing doors.

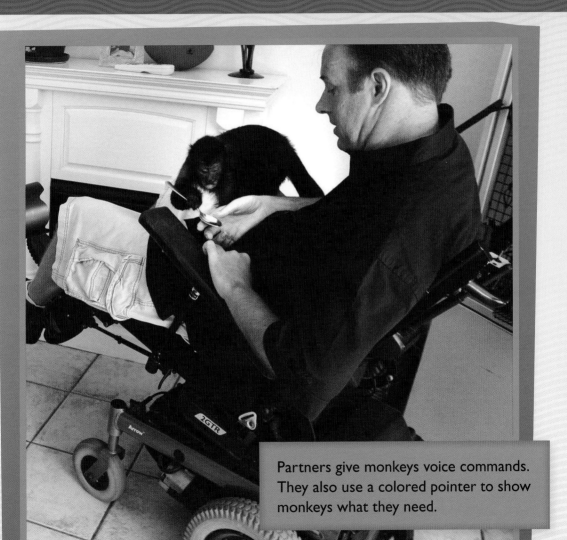

Partners give monkeys voice commands. They also use a colored pointer to show monkeys what they need.

Many capuchin monkey helpers are also friends to their partners.

Capuchin monkeys are well suited for being service animals. They like humans. And, they are small enough to sit on a person's shoulder. Some weigh only three to eight pounds (1.4 to 3.6 kg) as adults.

Capuchin monkeys can live to be 40 years old! They start training when they are teenagers. Their service careers can last 20 or 30 years. This is much longer than other types of service animals.

Did You Know?

In the late 1800s, capuchin monkeys often performed with street performers called organ grinders. The monkeys did tricks to entertain people and collect money. You can still see some organ grinder monkeys today.

Did You Know?

Most miniature horse trainers have worked with horses for at least ten years!

Hoofed Helpers

Even horses can be service animals! **Miniature** horses work with people who are blind. Like guide dogs, these guide horses are specially trained. They help keep their **partners** safe.

Miniature horses have a wide range of vision. They can see almost all the way behind them! This helps them guide their partners in busy public areas.

Guide horses wear sneakers because they walk on a variety of surfaces. Sneakers guard their feet and prevent slipping.

Miniature horses are well suited for service work. They are small and gentle. So, they are easy to control. They are also strong. Their **partners** can lean on them for help standing up.

Miniature horses live longer than dogs. Some live to be 50 years old! So, guide horses can work much longer than guide dogs.

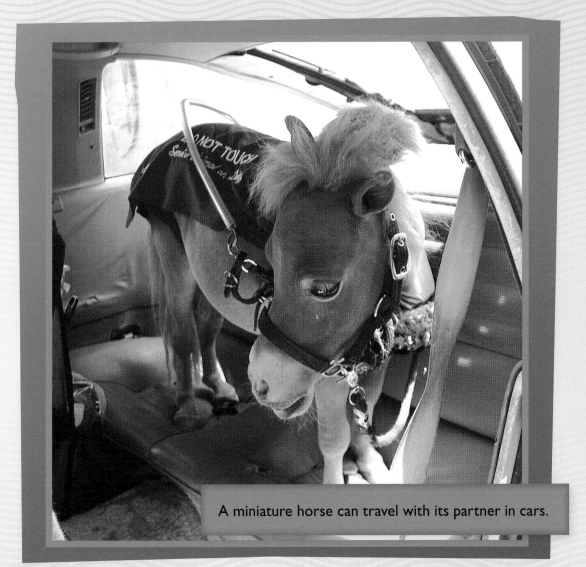

A miniature horse can travel with its partner in cars.

Did You Know?

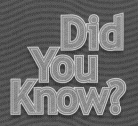

Gifted Workers

Service animals work to allow people to live more independently. Sometimes, they even save lives. Service animals do important work that improves the lives of many people!

A seizure dog notices when its partner is about to have a seizure. Then, it alerts its partner. Many times, this saves a person from injury or death.

The Animal Times

Starting Out

In 1999, the Guide Horse Foundation was started. It tests the use of guide horses as service animals.

First Service Monkey

Helping Hands is a national organization based in Boston, Massachusetts. In 1979, it trained and placed the first service monkey. Since then, Helping Hands has trained and placed more than 125 monkeys!

Important Words

alert (uh-LUHRT) to make someone aware of something.

deaf (DEHF) unable to hear.

harness an arrangement of straps used to hold on to or attach something to an animal.

injury (IHNJ-ree) hurt or loss received.

mental having to do with the mind.

miniature (MIH-nee-uh-chur) a smaller version of something else.

partner a part of a team.

physical (FIH-zih-kuhl) having to do with the body.

seizure (SEE-zhuhr) the physical signs, such as shaking and loss of body control, of a brain disorder.

spine backbone.

veteran a person who has served in the armed forces.

World War I a war fought in Europe from 1914 to 1918.

Web Sites

To learn more about service animals, visit ABDO Publishing Company online. Web sites about service animals are featured on our Book Links page. These links are routinely monitored and updated to provide the most current information available.

www.abdopublishing.com

Index